Behind Closed Doors

Ayesha Soomro

Presentation by *BookLeaf Publishing*

Web: www.bookleafpub.com

E-mail: info@bookleafpub.com

ISBN: 9789357442084

First edition 2023

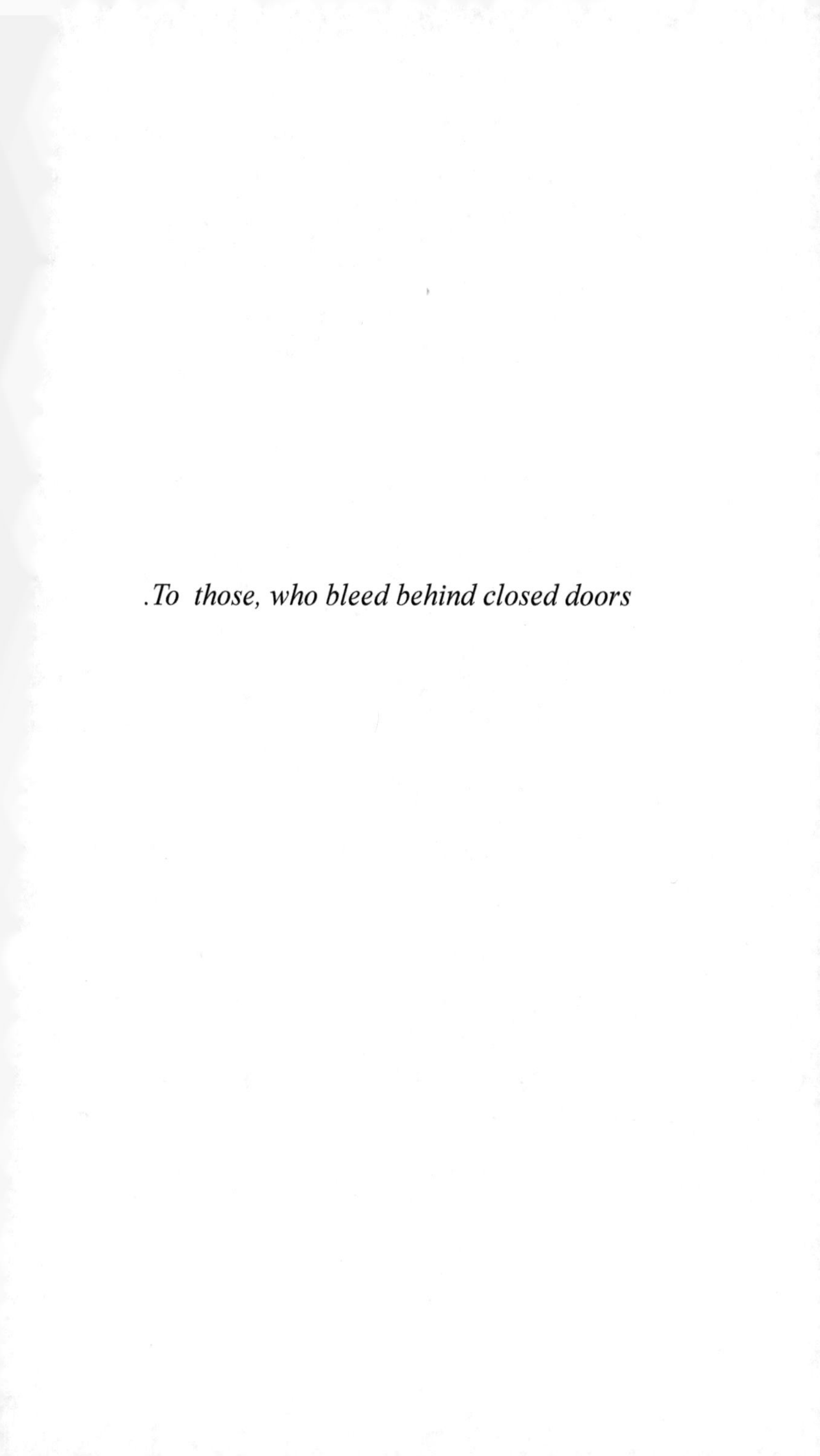

.To those, who bleed behind closed doors

ACKNOWLEDGEMENT

No one.

PREFACE

She spent sleepless nights behind those closed doors, the family slept and so did the dog she imagined, she wrote and wrote and bled.

How do you remember me?

Peppermints and toothpaste
Musk and burnt wood
Wet grass and crushed flowers
Cold water and the stars
Streetlights and umbrellas
Coffee and parchment paper
Grocery Stores and vintage fonts
Old books and the moon
Fairy lights and math
Music sheets and Urdu poetry
Candles and paintings
Persian songs and sweater vests
Kohl and literature
Strawberries and loyalty
Guitars and fast cars
Winters and vinyl
Black clothes and the rain
Anger and to-do lists
Blurred eyes and ink blots
Piano keys and big windows
Late nights and dreams that follow

In Everyhting

Luna

He smiled at me and said
"My light shines over many like you."

"If only you bled in the light"
"It's in the darkness, where the glint of your
metallic pains is
stronger
darker
heavier
and oh so much more dangerous than the ache
causer himself."

I thought to myself how you must be asleep,
 while the bruises of your words
 the iron bleed of your sugar promises
grew stale in the sun,
and the cruel soft moon
watched me every night
opening every wound in the stars
reliving every minute of it again.

The Prince

"Its expectations my love," he said, "beautiful betrayers, they are. Traitors, backstabbers, judases. Every tear of disappointment shed, is merely a rain of all the gorgeous chaos that our expectations cause. People kill, and some do it so beautifully, they leave you alive after, to suffer."
"To suffer and relive."

Venice

Two Decembers in a row.
Moondust and salt crusts.

Two Junes in a row.
Stardust and salt crusts.

She bid me goodbye when the tide was still
high.
Broken strings, broken rings.

Two Decembers in a row.
Moondust and salt crusts.

11/21/2021

I lay in her arms, as she played with a little blue flower on a clear night. It was her, me, and the meadow.

"How do you think one knows, when it's over"

" You don't"

"You don't?"

"No, if it was real, it's never really over. A fragment of them still lives."

"And does it hurt? Their living?"

"For each of us, it's different. It's when the fragment is no more a fragment it hurts. It's when it transforms into a shard that it's tragic. A shard from a mirror of kindness and eternal promises and illusions that hurts. It slashes right through you. Every vein in your beating heart feels it. Some days it's a stab, other times the wound bleeds for days. We fail to realize that some of us are bleeding inside. Burning bitter, faltering, regretting, reliving."

She got up, her face glistening with tears, and left.

There in the grass lay the debris of her abandoned love;

blue petals,

crushed.

She held me that day, and the meadow held her.

Would You Love Me?

If I told you I killed,
If I told you I hurt

Would you love me?

If I told you about my reasons,
If I told you about the seasons

Would you love me?

If I told you about the blood,
If I told you about his scars

Would you love me?

Grief

She's not the same anymore.
She screams a lot.
But she laughs a lot too.

She blames herself.
But she blames the others too.

She regrets a lot.
And she remembers a lot too.
She remembers and cries.
She remembers and sighs.

She remembers and screams a lot too.

She thinks about the last days.
She thinks about the first days.
She thinks about all the days.

She remembers a lot.

Stars fell apart

Stars fell apart

The only thing I remember is December

June comes every year

But the stars fell apart

Sometimes I write to understand

Sometimes I write to bleed a little less

It's ok mother I'm not going to end

Stars fell apart

Chase Atlantic

9

Oxygen Debt
Cocaine
God
Red lights
Molly
Depression
Saviours

Mother and Father

Im a bad person,
with bad grades

Im a bad person
with bad thoughts

Im a bad person,
with bad motives,

Im a bad person
Mother and Father arent

Flashbacks

I'll stay
Im here
Im not going
Lean on me

Bloody liar
Imagine being with someone whos so fricking
needy

18

From 6-9
The Sky was blue
Radio Waves and Bad Static

She was working 6-9
The sky was all the colors of the rainbow
Radio Waves and Pretty tunes

God's Children

Good Child,
you have suffered

There is light and you will find it...

Good Child,
you have cried

There is light and you will find it

The Bathroom Floor

Red more than the Grey Tile,
Dark more than the 18 light bulbs,
The Echo of silent screams more than the
Silence.

Third Degree burns of the day,
Fevers of Dissapointement,
Nirvana in her eyes
as she slept,

On The Bathroom Floor

Dont doubt Us

Us
Dont doubt it

Through the Maths and the rest of it

Us Dont Doubt it
Through hard guitar chords and burnt toast

Us
Dont Doubt it

Through me, you and the world

Emails

17 of them
Not one honest

17 of them
Not one of them true

17 of them
All of them lies

17 of them
All of them fake

17 of them
All of them full of all things untruthful

17 of them
17 of them

Not my Job

Telling you you look beautiful
Telling you its going to be alright
Telling you the world is yours
Telling you I love you
Telling you I love you
Telling you I love you
Telling you Im sorry
Telling you its Okay
Tellling you its going to be okay
Telling you things
Telling you stories
Telling you all of it
Telling you I love you

Telling you I love you

Vintage Broken Strings

New York 9 pm
Saturday Evenings
Subway Buzz

A Warm Dinner
Hands